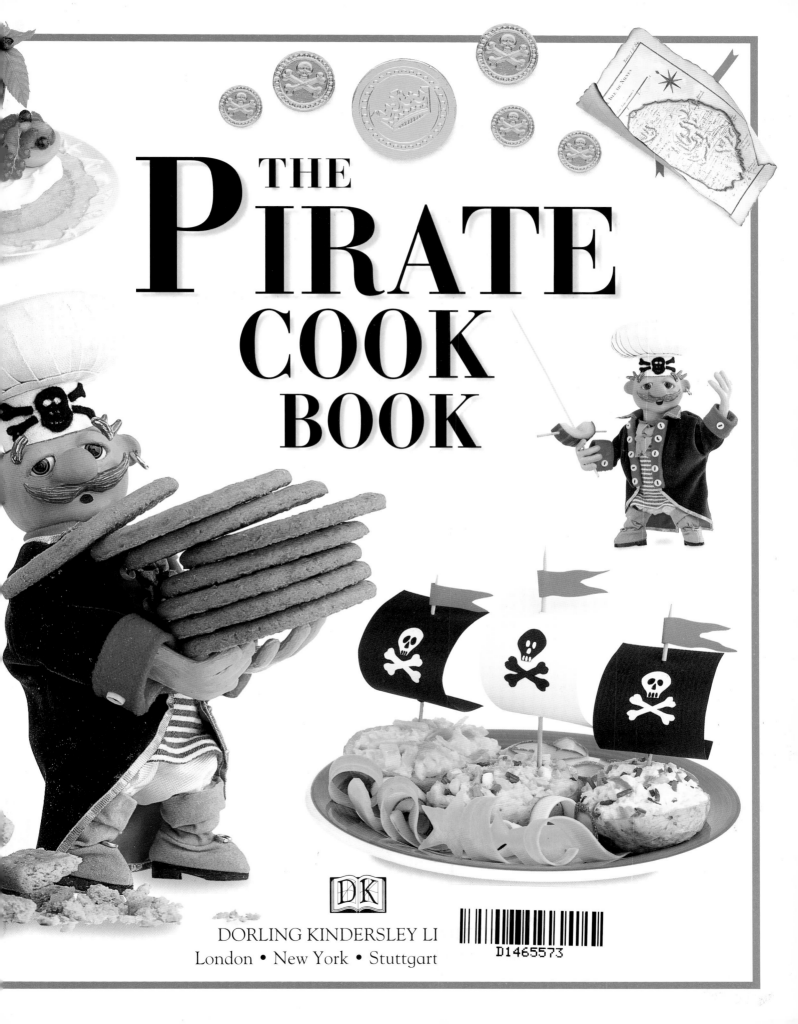

THE PIRATE COOK BOOK

DK

DORLING KINDERSLEY LI
London • New York • Stuttgart

D1465573

Galley Rules

1.  When the Jolly Roger is at full mast, an adult must be with you.

2. When the anchor is down, try some of your own ideas and ingredients.

3. Each recipe serves around four members of your crew.

4. Wash your hands before you start.

5. Wear an apron.

6. Collect all the ingredients you will need.

7. Be careful with sharp knives and always use a chopping board.

8. Wipe up spills and wash up as you go. Keep the decks clear.

9. Turn saucepan handles to the side so that you don't knock them off.

10. Use an oven glove to hold hot things.

Cooks' Tools

chopping board

knife

fork

spoon

wooden spoon

bowls

bun tin

grater

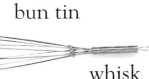

whisk

lolly moulds

baking sheet

blender

cookie cutters

jug

Techniques

Chopping

Place the food on a chopping board. Use a sharp knife to make downward cuts.

Grating

Hold the grater firmly and rub the cheese downwards against the grater. Keep your fingers out of the way.

Skewering

Skewer a chunk of food by pushing a wooden skewer through its middle.

Mixing

Put the ingredients in a bowl and stir together with a large spoon.

Whisking

Whisk egg whites by beating them quickly with a whisk until they are stiff and stand up in peaks.

Melting

Melt chocolate by heating it in a bowl over very hot water until it is liquid.

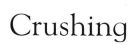

Crushing

To crush biscuits, put them in a plastic bag and beat with a rolling pin.

Blending

Use an electric blender or food processor to mix ingredients together well. Make sure that the lid is firmly closed.

Pirate Potato Boats

Jangling jellyfish, these'll warm your cockles.

You will need 4 potatoes 45g tuna 1 tablespoon mayo

30g sweetcorn 3 chopped spring onions  cheese

1. Set the oven to 200°C/ 400°F/Gas Mark 6.

2.  Wash  and prⁱck the potatoes with a fork. Wrap

them in

foil and p^op them in the oven.

3.  When the potatoes are

soft, ask an old sea-dog to help you

c_ut them in half.

4. Chop and **grate** the ingredients for the fillings.

5. Spoon the insides of the potatoes into bowls and mix with each one of the fillings.

6. Then drop the mix back into the potato skin.

Invent some fillings of your own.

7. Set sail on a feast of filled boats **bobbing** on a sea of salad waves.

Cut-Throat Kebabs
A sweet and savoury suprise on a stick.

You will need cheese  a selection of your favourite fruit
and vegetables cold cuts

1. chop all the ingredients into bite-sized chunks.

2. Take two wooden skewers and a fruit or vegetable chunk to **make** a sword just like mine.

3. Then pick and **mix** as you thread a selection of sweet and savoury treats.  Be **careful** not to stab your finger while you are doing it. Cut off the ends of the skewers.

4. Then they are ready for the **hungry** crew to eat. Just make sure you get some too.

Desert Island Dessert
For shipwrecked sailors with a sweet tooth.

You will need 2 egg whites   115g castor sugar   jelly

whipped cream   chocolate flakes   lots of fruit

mint leaves

1. Before you start, set your

oven to 120°C/250°F/Gas Mark 1/2.

2. Pop the egg whites into a

bowl and **whisk** them

till they stand up

stiff like white horses

on top of stormy waves.

3. Sprinkle in castor sugar, little

by little, while still **whizzing** your whisk.

4. plonk small blobs of mixture on to a baking sheet, making a well in the middle of each.  **Bake** for about two hours.

5. place the baked meringue on a sea of green jelly and **pack** a raft with fruits.

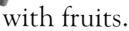

6. No desert island is complete without palm trees with chocolate trunks and mint leaf palms in a **blob** of cream.

Booty Bundles
Tuck into a sea-time treasure trove.

You will need 115g plain chocolate  115g butter

225g digestive biscuits 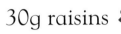 2 tablespoons double cream

55g glace cherries 55g flaked almonds

30g raisins

1. Crush the biscuits into tiny pieces.

Chop the cherries and mix them

with the nuts, raisins, and biscuits.

2. Ask an

ancient mariner to help you

melt

butter, cream, and chocolate

together over very hot water.

3. Mix the melted chocolate and biscuit mixture together.

4. Line the little bun tins with foil.

5. Dollop spoonfuls of mixture into the tray and pop it in the fridge.

6. When they are as cool as an iceberg, Scrunch the foil and tie it with string.

Your friends will think they have treasure for tea.

Titanic Treats

Jiggling icebergs, let's sink a few of these.

You will need orange juice lime juice melons

1. Press out sea creature shapes from the melon using nautical cookie cutters.

2. Lay the fruit shapes in the lolly moulds and fill the moulds with juice.

3. Be careful not to spill them as you pop them in the freezer for two hours. **4.** Hold them upside down

under a running tap for a few seconds and they will slide out.

Try other flavours of juice and different fruits for lots more titanic treats.

Tropical Tipples

Shiver me shakes, two juicy drinks.

Milkshake: 1 scoop ice cream   150ml milk   85g strawberries

Punch: 150ml cranberry juice   150ml orange juice

1 orange   1 apple   lots of ice

1. Wash and CHop some plump, ripe strawberries.

2. Plop all the ingredients into the blender.

3. Get an old sea-dog to screw the lid on tight and whoosh it all around till everything is blended.

1. Take orange juice and cranberry juice, **pour** them into a jug, and stir. **2.** Cut the orange and apple into slices. **Pop** the slices and some ice cubes into the juice too. ⚓ Serve these thirst quenchers to the crew with straws and extra fruit.

17

Shipmates' Snacks

It's a party. We'll have a whale of a time.

Fish snack: bread ▮ tuna ◯ mayo ◯ pepper ✕

cucumber ◯◯ radish ◯◯◯◯ olive ●

Nautical nibbles: bread ▮ cheese and ham ▮ olive ●

lettuce 🥬 cream cheese ◯ pepper 🫑

1. 🏴‍☠️ slice the bread in half. To make a fish shape, cut out two triangles for a tail and one for a mouth.

2. spread tuna mixed with mayonnaise all over the fish-shaped bread.

3. **Cut** the pepper thinly and arrange cucumber and radish slices on top like fish **scales**. Make an olive eye and pepper fins.

 Decorate black rye bread with a jolly roger **squeezed** from a tube of cream cheese.

 Grill a **cheesy** map on a piece of brown bread.

 Just copy this picture for a fine example of nautical **nosh**.

Dive - in Dips
Fine fodder for hungry sailors.

Pirate peppers: 3 peppers  115g hummus paprika

Dig-in dips: corn chips 115g guacamole 1 tomato

115g sour cream 1 avocado

Cannonball tomatoes: lots of cherry tomatoes cream cheese

1. Chop some peppers in half and scoop out the seeds. **2. Fill** the pepper halves to the brim with hummus. **3.** Make a stencil to mark an **X** of paprika.

1. Fill a bowl with guacamole and another with sour cream. Arm the crew with corn chips.

2. Load your corn chips till they overflow with diced tomato and avocado.

1. slice the tops off cherry tomatoes.

2. Scoop out the insides and then fill each tiny tom with cream cheese. **pop** its lid back on.

The Captain's Table